cats

understanding and caring for your pet

Written by
Claire Horton-Bussey

cats

understanding and
caring for your pet

Written by
Claire Horton-Bussey

Magnet & Steel Ltd

www.magnetsteel.com

Printed and bound in China through Printworks International Ltd.

ISBN: 978-1-907337-11-6
ISBN: 1-907337-11-3

Contents

Introduction

Cats are one of the most popular pets in the world – and it's easy to understand why. They are ideal for modern-living, requiring little money, space or time, compared to many pets, and, of course, they are incredibly adaptable, thriving in all sorts of households – single homes, busy families, older couples, country or town, apartment or mansion... Provided he is safe from roads and other dangers and can have his basic care needs met, a cat will make himself at home in many types of living arrangements.

Unlike dogs, cats can be left for hours while their owners work. They are small and do not require a large home or garden. Indeed, some are kept successfully as indoor house cats in places where road traffic is too hazardous.

This can work well with older, more sedate cats, provided they are given adequate opportunities to express their natural behaviours (hunting, climbing, scratching etc.) indoors.

Size also works in the cat's favour. They don't require large homes or gardens, they can be picked up and carried easily, are easy to take to the vet, they don't require masses of food, and they fit on a lap perfectly well for a cuddle!

They come in many colours and patterns, and, for those who would like even further choice, there are many pedigree breeds from which to choose, too. There really is a cat for almost every taste!

Taming the wildcat

Watch a cat playing in the garden or stalking a toy on the hearth-rug and it's not difficult to see where his origins lie. He may have been domesticated for several thousand years, but he still retains many features of his wild ancestor, the African wildcat (Felis sylvestrus libyaca).

The cat family (Felidae) is a varied group, and, in common with all carnivorous mammals, is thought to have descended from Miacids, which developed around 60 million years ago. By around 100,000 years ago, the cat family had evolved into Panthera (lions, tigers and other big cats), Acinonyx (cheetahs, who are unable to retract their claws), and Felis (smaller wildcats, such as lynx and the African wildcat).

The domesticated cat's story began with the agricultural revolution of the Neolithic Stone Age when humans began storing their crops. Rats and mice posed a serious threat to the reserves – and hence people's lives. Fortunately, cats were equally as attracted to the granaries – not for the grain but for the easy rodent pickings! People welcomed the cats' help in eradicating the rodents, and, over time, the cats became less fearful of humans and relaxed around the human settlements. As well as offering an easy source of food the settlements offered protection from wild predators that would have been fearful of humans.

A combination of some kind of genetic mutation occurring, together with selective breeding (with the people-tolerant cats in the settlement mating with others of a similar character), meant the cat became domesticated over time – although he is more than capable of reverting to the wild and surviving by his own wits if necessary.

His fortunes have waxed and waned through the ages, from being worshipped in Ancient Egypt to being persecuted in the Middle Ages for being thought of as the witch's familiar, but he is now securely top of our list of favourite pets.

How many?

It's often said that cats are solitary creatures, but this isn't strictly true. Yes, cats are solitary hunters, unlike some animals that hunt in pairs or packs, but they can live happily in groups. This is evident from watching feral cat groups, where close, lasting relationships can be seen, particularly in the adult females, who help to nurse and raise kittens together.

An only cat in a home will be more than content, provided his needs are met, but many cats can – and do – live happily with one or more of their own kind. The key to success is to ensure both cats are sociable and friendly and that each individual's needs are met (that they each receive plenty of petting, lap-warming, play and quiet time alone, where they can escape to a snooze spot away from others if they want to).

Most squabbles arise over competition for resources. So ensure that each cat has a litter tray, bed, food and water bowl, and 'high point' (somewhere such as a high windowsill). Remember, you also count as a resource, so make sure you give your lap and attention to each cat, too!

Personality also plays a part, of course. Some cats are simply loners and only you will know if your cat would accept a newcomer. Perhaps you have an oldie that has never shared his home with a feline friend and is aggressive to any cat that strays into the garden. Maybe you have a younger, very territorial cat or one that is very nervous and fearful. Such cats are generally in the minority, however. Most will accept a new cat in the home provided the situation is handled carefully.

- Scent is an important part of cat communication. Stroke one cat and then the other, rubbing under the cat's chin and his 'cheeks' at the sides of his mouth. Your hand will transfer the smell from his scent glands to the other cat. When they meet in the flesh, they will already be familiar with each other's scent and will already have a degree of familiarity.

- If you fear that they could become aggressive or chase each other, use a cat carrier to house the newcomer for the initial introductions, so they can get used to each other without any risk of harm.

- Introduce them before a meal-time, so they are hungry and easily distracted by food. Feed them in the same room but a good distance away from each other, so they don't feel threatened.

- Remain calm so the cats don't pick up any anxiety from you.

- Repeat the introductions little and often, until they are quite comfortable with each other. Then you can dispense with the carrier.

- Have some tasty treats to hand, such as slices of hotdog or diced chicken, and reward any calm behaviour.

With time, they will become increasingly confident around each other, and, in many cases, will be curling up next to each other for a nap before you know it!

Sourcing
your cat

Sourcing your cat

The best place to find an adult cat is from a reputable rescue centre. Here you will find a good selection of cats – perhaps even a pedigree – that have been vet-checked and handled and assessed by experienced staff. There are many types of rehoming organisations. Some rehome dogs and cats (and sometimes rabbits and other small pets, too), some just specialise in cats, and some are dedicated to just one breed, such as the Siamese.

If you want a rescue cat of a particular breed, you may have to wait some time for the right cat to become available, especially in the numerically small breeds, but if you would like a moggie, then you will be spoilt for choice.

Rescue centres are usually heaving with beautiful cats of every description. Some may be there because they have strayed and cannot be reunited with their owners, and some may be given up for rehoming because of a change in their owners' circumstances (e.g. moving to non-cat-friendly accommodation, emigrating, death or illness).

Where the cat has been handed in by the previous owner, you will know his full history. This is a great advantage in finding the right cat for your home and lifestyle. For example, if you have a dog and/or children, you can choose a puss that has previously lived happily with a canine and youngsters.

Where a cat's history isn't known – in the case of a stray, for example – the staff will assess him and place him accordingly. Some large centres have consultant behaviourists who can iron out any issues before rehoming, and all organisations should offer post-adoption support and advice should you encounter any queries or difficulties.

Every rescue centre has its own policies, but you will generally be interviewed, to assess your family and home's suitability and to find out your wants and needs. A home-check will also be performed. Not only will the home-checker be assessing any risks (e.g. how close your home is to a busy road) but the visit also gives them the chance of meeting all other family members (including children) and any other pets you have.

Most rescue centres ask for a suggested donation to cover the expenses incurred of neutering the cat, worming, flea treatments and any other vet fees.

Preparing
your home

Preparing your home

Before bringing your adult cat home, it's important that you prepare a room that puss can call his own. A small box room or spare bedroom is ideal. Cats, when stressed, seek small hiding places where they can feel safe and protected. Introducing him to your entire home and expecting him to settle in straight away is asking too much. First, get him used to the special 'cat room' and then, as he grows in confidence, he will venture out and start exploring the rest of the house in his own time, returning to his safe 'den' if spooked.

Place his bed, litter tray, and food and water bowls in the room, ensuring that the litter tray is as far away from the bed and bowls as it can be. Put some toys in the room for him to play with (or for you to play with together when you visit the room), and also put a scratching post inside. Make sure the windows are locked (some smart cats can open windows!) and ensure the room is cat-safe (no toxic houseplants, such as poinsettia or lilies; no irreplaceable heirlooms on a mantelpiece or shelf within the cat's reach, etc).

Next, cat-proof the rest of the house and garden. Assess each room from a cat's perspective, getting down on all-fours if necessary! Put breakable ornaments away or display them in a glass cabinet, and remove or put out of reach any toxic plants. Adult cats aren't usually as manic as kittens, who seem genetically programmed to find dangling wires to play with and chew, but some cats seem determined to find trouble wherever they are, so it's better to be safe than sorry and gather up excess electrical wire and fasten with a cable tie.

You should also discuss with all family members some basic rules to ensure the new cat's safety:

- The toilet seat should always be put down when not in use, so a curious puss can't jump in and/or drink from the bowl and ingest any harmful cleaning chemicals.

- Windows should be shut/locked and doors kept closed until the cat is allowed to go outside – and thereafter, all upstairs windows should be securely closed in case he jumps out. Screens can be fitted to windows that allow air to enter, but prevent a cat escaping.

- The washing machine and tumble-dryer doors should be kept shut when not in use and the insides should be checked before they are switched on in case puss has crept inside. All chemicals and medicines should be shut away (antifreeze, aspirin and paracetemol, for example, can be deadly to cats).

- The shed/garage should always be checked before being locked up, in case your cat has sneaked inside.

- Only use products that are entirely cat-safe in your garden.

- If you have a pool or pond, these should be covered and ramps should be fitted so that your cat can climb out if he falls in. As part of your preparations, you should also fit a catflap to the back door (unless you want to be pestered relentlessly to let the cat out and in and out again...) and set it to the locked position so your new puss can't yet escape into the big, wide world.

If you have a dog in your home, fit a stair-gate so your cat can have the upstairs to himself, away from any canine attention. In time, and with careful introductions, he will be happy to slip through the gate to commune downstairs, but in the early days, he will want to find his feet and settle in, unbothered by the family dog.

Essential
equipment

Essential equipment

A cat's needs are pretty basic compared with some pets, but there are some essential things you should shop for before bringing him home.

Bed

There is a bed to suit every taste and budget. Although you can get ornate four-posters and chaise longues for cats (yes, really!), most have humbler tastes, preferring a pile of freshly laundered washing! A simple, fleecy pad-type bed is a good starting point, or, better still, a hooded cat bed, which will help to make puss feel safe and protected. Place the bed in a corner of the room, or, if it is deep enough, on a windowsill.

Bowls

You will need at least two bowls – one for food and one for water – though four are ideal, so you have one being washed while another set is being used. Choose from plastic, ceramic or stainless steel. In the long-term, the last two are better options, as plastic bowls can eventually scratch and become quite abrasive. The design is important: cats prefer to eat from shallow bowls rather than deep ones.

Food

Find out in advance what the cat is fed, so you can get a supply before you bring him home. Most rescue centres will feed whatever has been donated, but some cats may have been handed in with specific food whims. Cats are known for being fussy – if you let them!

Litter accessories

Since the cat won't be allowed outside for a few weeks, while he finds his feet, you will need a litter tray, scoop, poo bags/nappy sacs, cat-safe disinfectant for cleaning, and a supply of cat litter. Even when he is allowed to go outside, you'll still need a tray for night-time use, as cats shouldn't be allowed out after dusk and before dawn for their own safety (cats are most in danger of road accidents when it's dark).

If you already have a cat, do still get another tray for the newcomer, as it is recommended that there is one tray per cat. For indoor house cats, who don't go outside, add a further tray – so two cats will need three trays between them.

A covered tray, whether with an open front or a cat-flap front, will help to control odours. Some even have filters in the top of the tray. Some cats prefer the privacy that a covered tray offers, while others can feel claustrophobic and prefer a standard 'open' tray. Bear in mind that the best way of keeping a sweet-smelling home is to scoop and change the entire litter regularly – whether the tray has a cover or not. If the litter is very dirty, most self-respecting cats won't use it and will find a clean corner of the house to relieve themselves instead!

There are many types of litter – wood-based pellets, paper, clay, silica crystals, lightweight, and the clumping type that forms a scoopable clump when it comes into contact with water. Find out what your cat is used to and get a supply before bringing him home. If you want to change the type of litter, add a little of the new stuff to the one he's used to already, mix it in, and gradually, over the course of a few days increase the amount of new to old until a complete change-over has been completed.

Tip: If your cat is fussy about the type of litter he uses, try a fine grain, which many cats prefer.

Identification

Most rescue centres will microchip the cats in their care before they are rehomed, but if you get your cat from another source, then you may have to arrange for your vet to do it. It is a simple procedure where a small chip, the size of a long grain of rice, is inserted under the skin at the back of the neck, between the shoulder blades. This chip contains a unique number, which will be held on a database with your details. If your cat becomes lost and is scanned by a reader, you can quickly be reunited. Occasionally, chips fail or migrate, so it is worth asking your vet to scan your cat at his annual check-up, to ensure it is still working properly. But the failure rate is very low and chipping has proved to be a very easy, reliable form of identification.

In addition, a collar and tag is useful so your cat can be returned to you without a scanner, and if it is made of reflective material, it could help improve your cat's visibility in low light.

It is very important that the collar is a safe one and will not strangle your cat if it is caught on a branch or something similar. A safety-clip collar that snaps open under pressure is a good option.

Scratching post

Scratching is an important part of feline behaviour. Expecting a cat not to scratch is entirely unreasonable, but scratching needn't be a problem – as long as you provide your cat with suitable places to perform the behaviour. If he has a scratching post in your lounge, placed at the right height and in the right position (see page 75), then he'll have no need to put his claws anywhere near your new sofa. Two or three posts should be sufficient for most homes, but you may need more if you have more cats, especially if they don't go outside very much.

Avoid carpet-covered scratching boards and posts – your cat might associate the material with the action and then begin scratching your floor coverings. Sisal is therefore preferable.

Toys

A good selection of toys is a worthwhile investment. If you spend time regularly playing with your cat, you will not only strengthen your relationship, but you'll also be helping to keep him active and stimulated (if bored, he might seek amusement by climbing your curtains, 'hunting' your shoelaces etc). Plus, playing with a cat is simply great fun and a fabulous way of de-stressing!

The range of toys available these days is astonishing, with everything from fishing-rod type toys and balls with bells to remote-controlled mice and multi-toy activity centres. There is something to suit every puss – and purse!

Whatever toys you buy, don't make every one constantly available to your cat. To keep his interest in them, put them away, and bring out a couple every day for him to play with. The next day, swap them with different toys. Rotating his toys will help to retain their novelty value for longer.

Also remember that toys don't play by themselves. Giving him a toy mouse might amuse him for a few minutes, but he'll soon lose interest if it's not wiggled to attract his attention, or thrown for him to chase and 'hunt'.

Feliway

Scent is very important to cats, not only as a means of communication to other cats but also in terms of a cat's personal sense of security. If a home smells of his own odour, he will feel far safer than in a new home where there are unfamiliar scents. Cats put their own smells on objects by rubbing their scent glands against them, particularly facial glands. This is why a cat will rub his head against the side of furniture, your legs, or against your hand while he is being petted.

Before you bring your new puss home, put a pheromone diffuser (Feliway) in his room and leave it on continuously for at least four weeks. This will reassure him and really help him to feel secure and 'at home'.

|Behaviour

Behaviour

Body language

The cat has lived alongside human beings for thousands of years and knows perfectly well how to make his feelings known to us. You don't have to be an eminent behaviourist to realise that when a cat is hissing, with his fur on end and his back arched, that he doesn't want to be stroked right now! Or that if he is purring loudly, eyes half-closed, and rolling on his back, rubbing against you, that he is enjoying being petted!

But there are some surprises. For example, a cat doesn't always purr from pleasure – it can also be a sign that he is in pain. Many injured cats or those giving birth will purr, as will dying cats.

Tail

A cat uses his tail for balance when climbing and cornering at speed and also to communicate. The tail will generally be held horizontally or slightly lower, but will be raised upright as a signal of a friendly greeting.

If he wags his tail, it's generally a sign of anger, or milder irritation if it's just the tip that is flicking.

Fur

A cat will fluff up his fur (known as piloerection) to make himself look bigger and fiercer. He also does it, to a lesser extent, when he's cold, with the hair trapping air against the skin. A cat's piloerection is similar to our own: we get goosebumps, with our body hair standing on end when we're cold or spooked, too!

Eyes

A long, slow blink is said to be a 'cat's kiss'; if a cat does this, it's usually a sign that he is very content and relaxed. By contrast, an aggressive cat will stare at its enemy. When playing or hunting, or if surprised, a cat's pupils will dilate, allowing the maximum amount of light to enter the eye. Cats are crepuscular, meaning they are most active at dawn and dusk, when they will rely on their ability to see movement in low light in order to hunt small prey.

Ears

If a cat is uneasy, he will flick his ears around, remaining alert to any sound that may signify danger. The ears flatten at the first sign of conflict, to protect them from damage in case there's a fight.

Posture

A cat will usually arch his back when he is fearful, to make himself look bigger when trying to ward off an aggressor. An aggressor might arch his back a little, too, to look as large and intimidating as he can.

A scared cat might crouch low when trying to escape a situation, as will a cat that is stalking prey. When you watch a cat hunt or play, you might notice that he wiggles his bottom before pouncing on a static object. This helps his eyes to pinpoint the exact position of the 'prey' and helps to ready his body, balance-wise, for the leap that will follow.

House training

The advantage of adopting an adult cat is that he is likely to be fully house trained already. But even untrained cats are very easy to teach. Thankfully, cats are very clean creatures, and, if you give them the right materials in the right places, they will pretty much train themselves! Put down a tray of litter in a quiet corner of the house (in the cat room you have prepared for him), show it to him and usually that's it. Job done!

If he does have accidents, then there's a reason why.

- Is the tray too close to his bed or food bowls? Understandably, cats don't like to toilet near where they sleep or eat.

- Perhaps the cat litter isn't pleasant for him to walk on (some cats don't like, for example, the wood-type pellets and prefer a fine-grain litter).

- Maybe there's not enough privacy and he doesn't feel secure to 'go'– perhaps because it's too busy and people are coming and going, or he's being stalked by another cat. So ensure there are plenty of trays dotted around the house in a multi-cat household, perhaps purchase a covered tray, and make sure the trays are in quiet corners and not busy thoroughfares.

- Is the tray clean? If you don't scoop poop promptly and change the entire litter regularly, the cat will find a cleaner place to relieve himself – such as a quiet spot behind your sofa.

- If you have an older puss, can he access the tray easily? Perhaps he can't get into the covered tray or finds it too much of a struggle to go down the stairs to get to it. Have plenty of shallow trays around the house.

- If he suddenly becomes incontinent, or, despite your best efforts, continues to have accidents, you must get him seen by a vet, as an underlying health issue, such as a urinary infection, may be responsible.

- Is the cat scent-marking rather than toileting? (see page 79 under Common Problems)

If your cat does have an accident, it is vital that the area is cleaned thoroughly, as the cat will otherwise be attracted back to the area to repeat his performance! Even if the area smells clean to you, the cat's sensitive nose will pick up any trace of scent and if you have used an ordinary household cleaner, the chances are it will contain ammonia or chloride, which are also found in urine and can tempt a cat back to the area! If an area smells of urine, who can blame him for thinking it's a toileting spot? Use a proprietary cleaner or a warm solution of biological washing powder (10 per cent) to wash the area, and then wipe with water and dry. Finally, go over lightly with an alcohol wipe or spray a fine mist of surgical spirit over, though this is not recommended for fabric surfaces. Do this cleaning routine on a small, unnoticeable part of the surface first, to check that it is safe to continue.

If your cat returns to the area out of habit, then move the furniture around so he can't get to the same spot again.

Note: Always wear gloves to change litter and to clean out the litter tray. Pregnant women and those with compromised immune systems should avoid handling litter because of the small risk of Toxoplasmosis, an infection caused by a microscopic parasite.

Outdoors

Outdoors

Letting your cat outside for the first time can be a nerve-wracking business. Unlike dogs, cats have their own life when outside and with this freedom comes inevitable dangers – from traffic, from curiosity (being shut in other people's houses, sheds or garages when being nosy), from being poisoned due to exposure to other gardeners' pesticides, or from eating a mouse or rat that has ingested toxins, or from other animals (not only getting into fights with other cats but perhaps stray dogs).

Other dangers come from being spooked by thunder or fireworks and running, petrified, until the cat is utterly lost.

This makes the outside world sound a terrifying place – and some people choose to keep indoor house cats only (see page 68). But, in truth, provided

you take some basic precautions, the risks are minimal and many cats reach a ripe old age, having lived a full and eventful life. Here are some points to remember:

- If you live near a busy road, puss will have to be an indoor house cat. Letting him outside really will be risking his life.

- Make sure you keep your cat in from just before dusk until after dawn.

- Put a high-visibility collar on him, to maximize his chances of being seen.

- Ensure your cat is neutered, to stop him fighting and copulating (not only to avoid unwanted pregnancies but also to avoid the diseases that are transmitted from such contact with disease carriers).

- Make your own garden as enticing as possible. For example, if there's a quiet, safe spot where he can snooze, and some trees he can climb or sit in (or an artificial observation spot, such as a DIY activity tree), then he is likely to spend more time in your garden.

Letting an adult rescue cat outside for the first time is less scary than releasing a reckless, foolhardy kitten who seems to think he's invincible. But it's important to take care nevertheless.

- The time that he should be kept indoors varies from cat to cat, with the general consensus being that when they try to get out, they are ready to go out. Certainly, keep puss in for at least three weeks, however, to give him time to bond with you and to imprint a sense of where his new home is. If he is still timid after this time, wait longer. Some cats need as long as three months; some are fully settled within a week and are raring to explore the great outdoors!

- Until he is ready to venture outside, ensure all doors and windows are closed and cat-flaps locked, and be careful when opening outside doors that puss can't make a run for freedom!

- When the day comes to introduce him to the garden, make sure the conditions are right. It should be a fine day (no threat of thunder storms that could spook him), not during firework season, and ideally with children at school (so you can fully focus on puss and he isn't distracted by them).

- Prepare something really appetizing, such as diced chicken, and ensure he doesn't have any breakfast before you let him outside.

- Open the back door and walk outside, calling him to you and showing the diced chicken. Give him a treat when he comes to you and make a fuss of him.

- Let him sniff around and explore the garden. Call him to you every few minutes and give him some chicken when he does so.

- After about 10 minutes, go inside, call him to you, give him the remaining chicken and then his meal.

- Short, frequent visits outside are best initially, so he gets used to coming inside and out, while venturing further each trip out. With each visit, you can gradually prolong the time that he's outside.

- Keep the back door open while he's out, so he has a fast, easy way back into the house in case he is spooked. Once you are confident that he knows his way back, close the door and make sure his cat-flap is unlocked.

Cat-flap

Adult cats usually know how to use cat-flaps, having encountered them in previous homes. If your cat hasn't used them before, he'll probably work it out for himself soon enough – it isn't rocket science, after all! But if your cat needs a helping paw, here's how to start from scratch:

- First, make sure the cat can easily access the flap. If it's too high for an elderly puss, for example he will struggle, or fail, to use it.

- Making sure it's unlocked, sit outside with some high-value treats – diced chicken, for example, with your puss inside, and call him through. If he noses the flap, praise him warmly and show the treats you have.

- If he uses the flap to get to you, reward him with the chicken and then switch positions, with you inside the house and him outside. Call him again and reward when he uses the flap to come inside.

- If he doesn't nose the flap, show him the chicken through the flap pane and call him encouragingly. If he still doesn't attempt to use it, arrange for a family member or friend to sit the other side of the door with the cat and to push the flap open so he can get to you – and his chicken reward!

- Once he's had a treat, he'll be eager for another, so repeat the exercise, this time with the helper opening the flap slightly less. Repeat, until the cat can use the flap without help.

House cats

Some people choose to keep their cats permanently indoors, because of the risks to the cat's safety; and some people have no choice – because of the cat's own health and risk to others.

For example, if you adopt a cat with a known health problem, such as FIV or feline leukaemia, your cat is at risk of passing on the disease to other cats and so will have to remain under your close control. Deaf cats, should also be kept indoors, for their own safety.

With a house cat, you have to work extra hard to ensure your puss's needs are met within the confines of your home. If he is deprived of opportunities to express his natural behaviour – hunting, climbing, scratching, etc – he will become bored and unhappy, and serious behavioural problems can develop.

- Is he sociable? Would he enjoy a feline playmate?

- Play with him as much as you can throughout the day, using a variety of toys to maintain his interest.

- Set aside time for regular training sessions. Cats are very intelligent and take well to clicker training. Using his brain will keep him mentally alert and stop him stagnating – plus it's fun and strengthens the pet/owner bond.

- Kitty Kongs, stuffed with catnip, or puppy Kongs stuffed with pate or cheese will keep him amused.

- Indoor grass (from pet shops) is a must for a house cat. Cats enjoy nibbling grass and it's thought to provide essential roughage to prevent constipation and to allow furballs to be brought up.

- Consider building (or having built) a pen that he can access from the house – where he can feel the wind in his fur and watch the world go by.

Behaviour:
Common
problems

Behaviour: Common problems

Cats are pretty straightforward creatures and rarely suffer behavioural problems. But if they haven't been raised well and thoroughly socialised, or if their basic needs are not met, problems might develop.

Often it is simply a matter of understanding why the cat is behaving as he is (perhaps he is being destructive due to boredom, for example), and providing him with what he is lacking (in this case, more varied, stimulating play and opportunities to exercise his mind and body). But if you are unable to deal with a problem, do not hesitate in contacting the experts, as behaviour issues can escalate quickly. The sooner a difficulty is dealt with, the better! Your vet will first check that there is no underlying health issue responsible for the problem, before referring you to a suitable expert – one that is qualified and experienced in dealing with cat behaviour in a kind, non-punitive, reward-based manner.

Scratching

Scratching *per se* isn't a problem; it's a necessary feline behaviour. Cats need to scratch to sharpen up their claws (the outer husk is removed through scratching, revealing a new, sharp point beneath), to deposit scent from the footpad (surrounding his territory in his own scent, making it feel familiar and safe to him, as well as communicating to other cats that the area has been staked), and to stretch and exercise his muscles.

Scratching only becomes a problem when it is performed at an inappropriate place – against the arm of the sofa, for example, instead of on the designated scratching post.

There are several reasons why a cat might be scratching inappropriately.

- Does he have enough posts around the house? If he does, are they in the right locations? Cats often scratch at key strategic points in the home, often by doorways. Try moving his scratching trees/posts around, bringing them close to where he is already choosing to scratch, so he has an alternative to your sofa or bed!

- Do the posts tick the right boxes? Are they upright, steady, and fixed at the right height for your cat?

He should be able to reach up at full stretch. Sisal or bark are the best coverings – certainly not carpet! If the posts are old, do they need to be recovered? If your cat can't get a good purchase on a post, he could seek an alternative outlet for his claws...

- Is it an attention-seeking behaviour? Forbidden scratching is a sure-fire way of getting an owner's attention – and once your cat has that, he can lead you to the back door or the food bowl, or get you to play with him, or roll over for a tummy tickle... Ignore inappropriate scratching entirely – and instead encourage him to use posts, giving oodles of attention when he uses the right place!

- Sometimes scratching in a particular place has already become a habit, usually from when he was a kitten, before he was let outside. To encourage your cat to scratch against fences, trees and gate posts outside, ignore any indoor scratching and encourage him to use indoor scratching posts by tying bark to them and sprinkling with catnip. If he gets used to the sensation of scratching against outdoor textures, he will eventually transfer his scratching to the garden.

- Is he stressed? Is he scratching to immerse himself in his own scent? Does a pheromone diffuser help to calm him?

Unless the cause of stress is obvious (perhaps a new puss has joined your home) it would be advisable to get him checked by a vet, in case there's an underlying medical reason for the anxiety. If he's fit and well, the vet might refer you to a behaviourist.

Tip: To discourage inappropriate scratching, apply double-sided sticky tape to the forbidden areas. He won't like the sensation on his paws and will therefore be more likely to use the scratching post you've provided for him.

Scent marking

This shouldn't be confused with toileting (eliminating), where the cat will generally squat and empty his bladder. With scent marking, however, the cat usually stands with his tail up, and sprays just a millilitre or two on to a vertical surface (such as a gate post, door, table leg). Occasionally a cat squats to deposit a small amount of urine on to something horizontal, such as a bed, or leaves faeces there (known as middening). In all cases of scent marking, the scent (be it urine or faeces) will be left uncovered, whereas the cat will try to cover his 'business' if toileting.

Scent is an important form of communication between cats and they will often scent mark outside to mark the boundaries to their territory.

So scent marking is a normal feline behaviour – but it's not something we appreciate when it's done in our homes!

A cat might mark indoors to make it smell familiar, if he is feeling insecure. Is there an obvious cause for the behaviour – for example, a recent move or a new pet joining the home?

If there is, then a Feliway diffuser or spray might help to boost his confidence while he settles into his new home or you address the cause of his anxiety.

Does he have enough places of security – places to which he can retreat if visitors come, children are too noisy, or other pets are too boisterous? Can he 'be a cat' to the full? Can he use all his senses and energy, to scratch, play, hunt and explore?

Is he feeling insecure due to pain or ill-health? There could be an underlying health issue that needs investigating by your vet.

If you cannot find the cause of the stress or you need help to address it, then seek a referral to a behaviourist.

Toileting

If your cat is incontinent in the house (and you're sure the behaviour is not scent marking, then it's a case of starting from scratch and checking all the basics are in place: that you have the right tray and cat litter and sufficient numbers of trays in the right location. Make sure they are scooped and changed regularly, and that your cat doesn't have a health issue that is responsible for the accidents.

Nervousness

Early socialisation is so important for a kitten to grow into a happy, confident adult cat. But if you've adopted a rescue puss, who is already an adult, is it too late? Will you always have a nervous cat? Not necessarily. Cats, like people, have different personalities depending on their genes, upbringing and life experiences, and some cats are more outgoing than others. But a nervous cat can be helped to be more confident. Some cats just need a few days, weeks or months to settle into a home and assess the situation, and all family members, before realising they are safe and coming out of their shell.

Others need a little more help. Although they might never be bombproof and outgoing, you might be able to boost their confidence a little with the use of a Feliway diffuser or spray, and ensuring he has plenty of bolt-holes to use if he needs to escape a stressful situation.

Showing him that he can trust you and gently socialising him is also worth trying. Put an indoor crate in a corner of the living room, covered with a blanket and with some familiar bedding inside so it creates a cosy den. Use a Feliway spray or diffuser in the room. Give him tasty treats when he's in the crate, so he learns to associate the place with enjoyable experiences. Ask a cat-loving friend or family member to visit at a pre-arranged time – and ensure the cat is in the living room, with all exit routes blocked, so he cannot escape and avoid the situation. The friend can feed the cat with treats if the cat is calm enough to accept them. If not, don't force the issue; just being in the same room as a 'stranger' is a good first step. Over time, very gradually, with repeated encounters with cat-friendly visitors, the cat's confidence should grow as he realises that no harm will come to him.

If you need help devising a programme to follow, contact a reputable behaviourist. Remember: a steady, patient approach is best – if you rush, all progress can be lost.

Food

Food

Most cats will eat whatever they are given – but some are prone to being fussy, particularly if allowed to become that way when younger, with an owner replacing perfectly fine, if bland, cat biscuits with succulent chicken or tuna the moment a cat, for whatever reason, isn't interested in finishing his meal that day. It doesn't take long for a canny puss to realise that refusing a meal results in finer fare being offered!

If you adopt an adult cat, try to discover what food the previous owners or rescue centre were feeding. A sudden change in diet can cause diarrhoea, and this, together with the stress of a house move and settling in with a new family, can put considerable strain on the body. If you want to change the cat's diet, wait at least a few months, until he's settled, and do it gradually, over the course of a week to 10 days, replacing a little of the cat's ordinary food with the new type, until, eventually, a complete changeover has been achieved.

Types of diet

There is now a type and flavour of food to suit every taste and budget – and there are even veterinary diets for specific health issues. In a nutshell, there are basically dry and wet foods to choose from. Dry diets are usually 'complete' – meaning they provide all the nutrients needed for a cat's good health, and no supplementary foods are needed. Crunching on the hard biscuits can be beneficial to a cat's dental health (as opposed to wet foods that stick to the teeth), and they don't go 'off' or attract flies as wet foods can.

Wet food is smellier, messier but often highly attractive to cats, and is preferable for oldies who might not have the teeth necessary to crunch dry food. It is also a good option where you need to tempt a cat's appetite, or where the cat is prone to feline lower urinary tract disease (FLUTD).

Wet and dry foods usually come in different lifestage varieties, to cater exactly to a cat's changing needs – with kitten, adult, indoor-cat, and senior varieties available.

Feeding times

Dry food can be put out in the morning and left throughout the day for the cat to graze on. Follow the amounts recommended on the packaging, which will be dependent on your cat's weight. Or you can divide his daily amount into a couple of portions, which you put down for him morning and evening. This might be preferable if you have a multi-cat household where one greedy puss might tuck into other cats' meals if not monitored.

Wet food should not be left out all day, as it will attract flies and go off. Tins are available, though pouches of food are more popular and mean that every serving is fresh. Lids can be put over an opened can of food, but some cats are so fussy that they will not be keen on finishing the contents at the next meal time!

Drinks

Fresh drinking water must be available at all times – and is especially important if the cat is fed an all-dry diet. Some cats prefer running water – many a puss will be found pawing at a dripping tap – and pet drinking fountains are available for such water babies.

Cat milk can be bought in small bottles from supermarkets or pet stores, but do not be tempted to give cow's milk to your cat. He'll lap it up happily, but he will not be able to digest the lactose (milk sugar) and could well suffer an upset tummy.

Grooming

Grooming

Most cats are short-haired moggies that require minimal coat care, being perfectly equipped to groom themselves. Their rough tongues brush through the coat, distributing natural oils through it and removing dead hair.

But that's not to say they don't need a helping hand. A brush through once a week will help to prevent the build up of furballs as well as minimising the amount of dead hair that is left around the house on carpets, clothing and furniture. It will also help with the pet-owner bond and give you the chance to look for any parasites in the coat and for any physical changes that need to be investigated by a vet, such as any lumps or scratches.

Some breeds need more assistance, though, particularly where humans have 'interfered' with the original cat design. For example, the Persian's coat is now so long and thick that the cat would not be able to keep it in good condition without human help.

A Persian would be a matted mess in a very short time if left to his own devices.

When you buy or adopt your cat, the breeder or rehoming centre should give you specific advice on the care that your cat's coat will need.

Routine

Getting a cat used to grooming when still a kitten is ideal, but it's easy enough to get an adult puss used to being brushed and combed if you simply incorporate it into an ordinary petting session. Stroke him all over and, when he's relaxed and purring, simply begin to brush him gently (keep your grooming tools by your favourite armchair, so they are in easy reach!). Brush for just a couple of minutes, give him a treat and then simply stroke him with your hand again. Later, try a couple more minutes. Keep sessions short and frequent, and very gradually extend them in terms of time and the areas groomed.

Use the services of a professional groomer if you don't have the time or expertise. If your cat would be stressed by the car journey or visit to a salon, find a groomer that will visit your home.

- Cats don't only groom to keep themselves clean; it also helps to cool a cat in warm weather, with the saliva evaporating from the coat, and distributes oils to waterproof the individual hairs.

- Grooming is an important bonding activity between pet and carer – and between friendly cats, too.

- A cat usually grooms when calm and content, but he might also groom as a diversionary behaviour or if stressed. A cat that over grooms will need to be seen by a vet, who will refer to a behaviourist if necessary.

- Any change in coat should be reported to your vet, as hair loss or a change in texture may be indicative of a health issue.

Health

Health

Cats are pretty robust, healthy creatures, but there are times when they will need veterinary intervention. The sooner this intervention comes, the better the chances of recovery;

Be alert to signs of ill-health so that you can contact your vet at the earliest opportunity. Look out for any change from your cat's usual healthy condition and normal behaviour. If he is sleepier than usual; drinking or eating more or less; if he is grooming more; if he is grumpy or less tolerant of being petted... all of these signs can suggest that something is wrong. More obvious signs are the physical changes: perhaps there's a change in the type and frequency of his toileting habits; perhaps there's a change to his coat, his eyes and/or nose are runny, or he is scratching himself. Has he lost or put on weight? Does his breath smell? Have any lumps appeared?

All of these signs can be spotted quickly if you spend time with your pet, and instinct often kicks in, too. "I can't put my finger on it, but my cat just doesn't seem himself" is commonly heard at vet practices around the country, and, from there, the vet can examine the animal for any leads.

Do not ever be tempted to treat the cat yourself. Many drugs intended for humans – such as paracetemol – are highly toxic to cats. A visit to the professionals at the first sign of illness often means a condition can be treated quickly – and more affordably.

Pet insurance is worth exploring, as unexpected vet bills can be difficult to find – particularly if, given veterinary advances, specialist treatment is given or a chronic, long-term condition emerges. Do be aware of the different types of policy when researching insurance, as some policies only give 12 months' cover for each condition.

Vaccinations

With adult cats that have been rescued and where the health history is unknown, most vets advise starting from scratch and treating your adult like a kitten – on the assumption that the cat hasn't had any vaccines. If you do have a complete health record for your cat, then continuing with annual boosters will suffice.

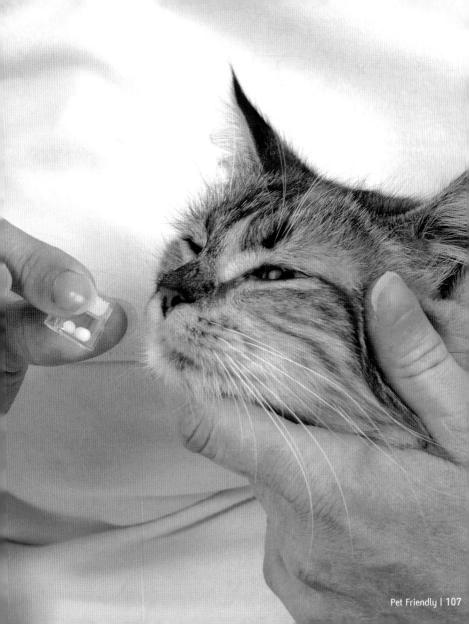

You should research the issue and discuss any concerns with your vet, who will have local knowledge and be able to assess your own cat's lifestyle, health and background and help you to come to a decision based on this risk assessment.

Do note that it is important, when adopting an adult rescue of unknown past, to be sure of the cat's health – vaccinating against feline leukaemia, for example, is all well and good, but how do you know that your cat doesn't already have it? Ask the rescue centre about its screening policy before you fall in love with a puss. Otherwise, you could end up adopting a cat who could fall ill months later, costing you hundreds of pounds and possible heartbreak – not to mention risking the health of any other cats in the household or neighbourhood in the meantime. If you consider that diseases are often passed on by fighting or copulating, you can see how stray unneutered toms and queens are at particular risk.

Parasites

Ectoparasites live on the skin; endoparasites live inside the body. The most common parasites that affect cats are fleas, ticks and mites (ectoparasites) and roundworms and tapeworms (endoparasites).

They can all be picked up easily from other cats and/ or the environment, so it's important that regular defleaing and deworming is part of your care routine. Seek your vet's advice about which products to use (some over-the-counter preparations may not be as effective), and ask about dosage and frequency.

Fleas

Fleas are small, dark, wingless insects that can jump very high – the equivalent to an adult human clearing around 900 feet! Once they leap on to your cat, they can go undetected in the fur, laying eggs and reproducing at an alarming rate before you suddenly become aware that you have an infestation – not just on the cat, but in your home, where eggs will have fallen off and hatched in the carpets, gaps in the floorboards and so on. It's said that for every flea you find on your cat, there will be many more in the home, so as well as treating the cat, it is important, if you find fleas, to remove them from the environment.

Often, you will notice small black specks – the flea dirt – in the coat before noticing the actual fleas. If you groom your cat on a large sheet of white paper, you might notice the specks more easily, as they will fall on to the sheet. Once wetted, the specks will dissolve into red – the blood that the flea has fed on.

Flea treatments for cats include collars, powders, sprays, spot-ons (drops that are applied to the back of the neck) and tablets (which interrupt the flea's breeding cycles). Some people swear by natural repellants, too. It is important to follow your vet's advice, as otherwise a dangerous toxic reaction may occur.

Ticks

These can be picked up in long grass. They latch on to the cat's skin and, like fleas, feed on the cat's blood. They swell in size as they feed and eventually drop off. They should be removed carefully, to ensure their contents are not squeezed back into the cat and to also avoid keeping the head/mouthparts embedded in the cat, when infection can occur. A tick-removal tool can be bought from your pet shop or vet surgery; if you are unsure of how to use it, ask your vet or vet nurse to show you how. Do be aware that ticks can spread disease – not only to other animals but sometimes people, so report any adverse effects following a bite to your doctor or vet.

Flea treatments often kill ticks, too; ask your vet for advice.

Mites

Head-shaking and scratching at the ear can be signs that there is something wrong with the ear – either an infection of some sort, or the presence of earmites. Your vet will diagnose and treat accordingly.

Tiny red insects might be found in the late summer, early autumn called harvest mites. These can cause intense itching and a red, spotty reaction.

Biting lice can also be found on feline coats – particularly where the cat is under the weather and has a compromised immune system. The lice are visible with the naked eye, though you might notice a change or loss of coat first.

As ever, seek veterinary advice for a diagnosis and treatment.

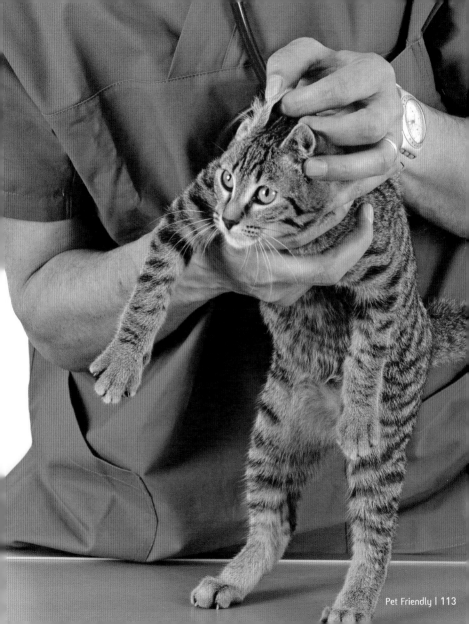

Worms

A cat with fleas can get tapeworms simply by grooming himself. Put simply, flea larvae eat tapeworm eggs. If a cat swallows a flea when grooming, the tapeworm can develop inside him.

You might not know your cat is infected unless the worm burden becomes heavy, resulting in ill health

If your cat uses an indoor litter tray (as he should, at least at night, when he is kept indoors), then you might see segments of the worm in the faeces, or you might spot them on the cat's bedding. They will look like small rice grains.

Roundworms can also be a problem, with the eggs passing to other pets or, rarely, people by ingesting egg-infested faeces. Hunting cats are prone to these and to tapeworms, from ingesting rodents that are infected. Kittens are often infected, with the larvae of roundworms passing to them via their mother's milk. A pot-belly, poor condition and tummy upsets can often indicate a heavy burden.

Routine worming is advised. Frequency and dosage will depend on the preparation used and your cat's lifestyle, but is generally every three to six months. Your vet will give you specific advice according to the treatment he or she recommends.

Fat cats

Many cats will not over-eat, but some cats will happily munch their way to obesity. Rescued cats that were once strays, for example, might eat and eat when food is available, storing up food in readiness for a future 'famine'. Other cats are just greedy! Older, less active cats can put on weight simply by being less active – and the same applies to indoor house cats and neutered moggies that will roam less. It's important to ensure that your cat is given lots of opportunity to play and exercise, not only to burn calories but also to avoid boredom. If a cat's only pleasure in life is eating, he'll quickly become obese.

It's not just quantities of food that can cause a cat to put on weight; the type of food can also be inappropriate. Feeding cream to your puss, instead of cat milk or water, for example, isn't going to do his waistline any favours – nor his health.

Your vet will help you monitor your cat's weight and devise a weight-loss programme, having first established that there are no underlying health issues causing the problem.

Accidents/ first-aid

Cats really do seem to have nine lives, managing to get into – and out of – all sorts of scrapes. But that's not to say that they are invincible. It's important to be safety-conscious and also to be prepared for emergencies. Keep the cat-carrier in an easily accessible place (not hidden at the back of the garage under a ton of unused garden furniture or in far recesses of the loft), so you can find it, put the cat inside and drive to the vet surgery as quickly as possible if your cat needs urgent medical treatment. Write the number of your veterinary surgery on the fridge door, by the phone, or somewhere else that's visible and immediately obvious. Keep a pen and piece of paper close by in case you need to write down the details of the out-of-hours emergency contact.

There are plenty of good first-aid sites on the internet that are worth reading, so you are fully prepared for any future emergencies.

Neutering

Neutering involves removing the testes in males and the ovaries and uterus in females. Neutering your cat is essential, to avoid unwanted pregnancies and to protect his or her health. When so many perfectly healthy cats and kittens are being destroyed for want of a home, breeding a litter of moggies is unforgivable. Even if you have homes for the anticipated kittens, by producing a litter, you will be condemning to death shelter cats that could have been rehomed instead.

Neutering a cat will also prevent spraying in toms, calling in queens and stop them acquiring sexually transmitted diseases. Toms often fight when competing for a mate, too, and are then at risk of diseases such as calicivirus, FIV and feline leukaemia, for example. Unneutered cats are at increased risk of road accidents, too, as they roam further in search of a mate and are single-minded in their pursuit – to the detriment of their road-sense.

Reputable rehoming agencies will neuter healthy adult rescued cats before they are adopted.

Losing
your cat

Losing your cat

Sadly, cats do not live as long as humans and the time will come when your cat dies or has to be put to sleep.

Choosing when to euthanase your cat has to be one of the hardest decisions you'll make – and is also one of the most important. You have a duty of care to ensure that your cat has a good quality of life. If he is in pain, with no hope of recovery, your vet will suggest that he is put to sleep and you should be guided by his or her professional opinion.

The procedure is done by injecting barbiturates into the cat's vein so that he loses consciousness and dies. It is painless for the cat – though terribly painful, in emotional terms, for the devoted owner he leaves behind.

While your cat is young and healthy, it is important to consider what you would like done after your cat is put to sleep, as you never know what is around the corner. Perhaps he will die suddenly in an accident – and you will have to make snap decisions, at a highly emotional, stressful time, which you might later regret. Do you want to take the cat's body home to bury in your garden, perhaps under his favourite tree or sun-bathing spot?

Perhaps you want him to be buried in a pet garden of remembrance, so that you can visit him, regardless of whether you move home. Perhaps you want him cremated, individually or in a group, and want to scatter his ashes or keep them in a commemorative container. Would you like the vet to visit your home and have him put to sleep in familiar surroundings, or would you prefer to take him to the vet clinic to have it done?

Consider all these aspects when you don't need to, and it will help when the heartbreaking time finally does come.

Finally, if you have never experienced the death of a much-loved pet before, you might be taken aback by the strength of your feelings. It is perfectly normal to feel utterly devastated at losing an important member of your family – and it is not unusual for the grief to be overwhelming. Do cry when you need to, talk about your cat with others who knew him, and perhaps seek support from a pet-loss group on the internet. Some animal welfare groups also run befriender schemes where you can talk to trained counsellors about your grief.

Be assured that, eventually, your tears will be replaced with smiles as you remember your special friend and recall the happy times you shared together.

Weights & measures

If you prefer your units in pounds and inches, you can use this conversion chart:

Length in inches	Length in cm	Weight in kg	Weight in lbs
1	2.5	0.5	1.1
2	5.1	0.7	1.5
3	7.6	1	2.2
4	10.2	1.5	3.3
5	12.7	2	4.4
8	20.3	3	6.6
10	25.4	4	8.8
15	38.1	5	11

Measurements rounded to 1 decimal place.